Jonathan Cape
Thirty Bedford Square
London

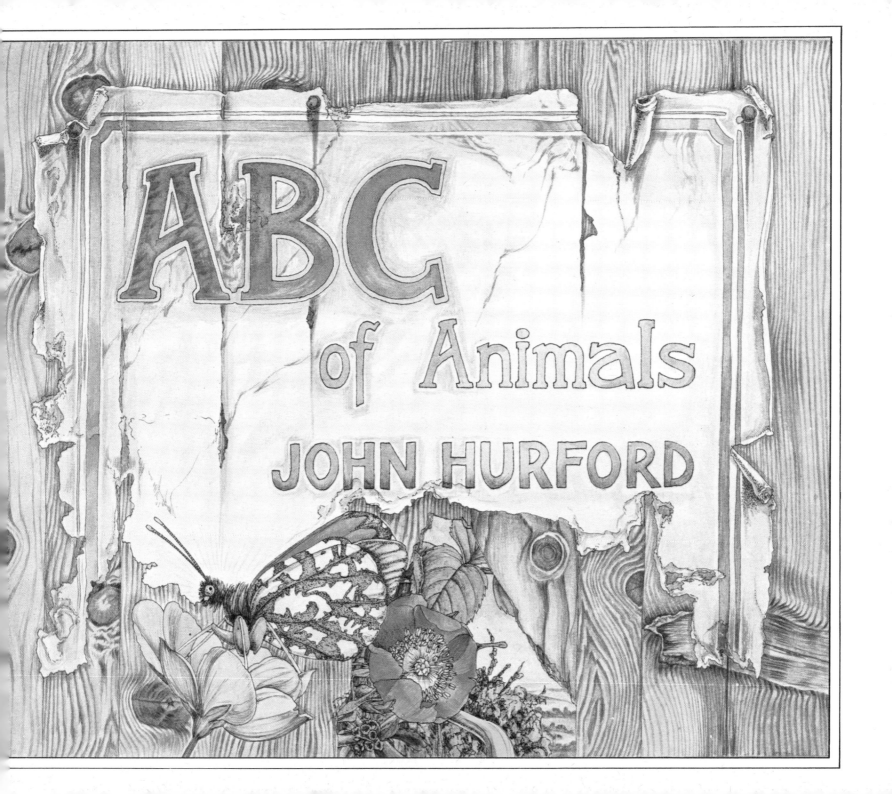

A is for Alligator

B is for Buffalo

C is for Camel

D is for Dolphin

F is for Fox

G is for Gorilla

H is for Hare

I is for Impala

K is for Kangaroo

L is for Lion

M is for Moose

N is for Nuthatch

O is for Orang-utan

P is for Panda

Q is for Quail

is for Rhinoceros

S is for Squirrel

T is for Tiger

U is for Uakari

V is for Vulture

W is for Warthog

Oryx ends with X

Y is for Yak

First published 1975
© John Hurford 1975
Jonathan Cape Ltd, 30 Bedford Square, London WC1

ISBN 0 224 01175 8

Printed in Great Britain by
Tindal Press, Chelmsford, Essex